LINKIN PARK

THE UNAUTHORISED BIOGRAPHY

IN WORDS AND PICTURES

A CATALOGUE RECORD FOR THIS BOOK IS AVAILABLE FROM THE BRITISH LIBRARY.

ISBN 184240 159 9

TEXT BY **BEN GRAHAM**
EDITED BY **BILLY DANCER**
ART DIRECTION AND DESIGN BY **A CREATIVE EXPERIENCE, LONDON**

PRINTED AND BOUND IN THE UK.

CHROME DREAMS
PO BOX 230
NEW MALDEN
SURREY KT3 6YY
UK

LINKIN PARK

THE UNAUTHORISED BIOGRAPHY

IN WORDS AND PICTURES

CHROME DREAMS

www.chromedreams.co.uk

CONTENTS

t is rare for a fully formed band to appear, apparently from nowhere, and achieve immediate commercial and artistic success. t is rarer still in the field of alternative rock and metal, where traditionally artists have to be seen to have paid their dues gradually climbing from obscurity to respect and recognition. And it is almost unheard of for a young band to hit paydirt with a debut album that sounds like no one else, yet has obvious mass appeal. But this is exactly what has happened to Linkin Park, a band that, from day one, have been accused by the media of being fakes. Yet paradoxically, much of Linkin Park's appeal stems rom the fact that they are actually one of the most honest groups in rock music today.

Alternative bands are supposed to struggle on the live circuit for years before eventually scraping enough cash together to release a string of limited edition singles on an obscure independent label. Then maybe a handful of albums, each one selling marginally more than the last, while still remaining well out of reach of the charts. Gradually, though, they receive critical attention and underground radio play, building up a following through word of mouth and magazine coverage, as the fans and the writers pride themselves on being the first to discover this hot new act. Maybe, eventually, there is a breakthrough hit, at which point the hardcore cry "Sell out!" and turn away. Alternatively, a band can become huge purely by virtue of album sales and incessant touring, thus attaining commercial success without any perceived artistic compromise.

Linkin Park, though, have done things differently. Their first album release, *Hybrid Theory*, seemed to leap straight out of the blue and into the upper reaches of the Billboard Charts, going double platinum in the US within six months. Their life on the road had only just begun when they found themselves bona fide pop stars, with the album reaping no less than three mammoth hit singles. Tracks like "One Step Closer", "Crawling", and "Papercut" boasted not only hip-hop beats and raging guitars, but soaring, radio-friendly choruses, deft rapping and lyrics that were at once angry, intelligent, introverted and had something to say. Crucially, they have never resorted to swearing in their songs as a lazy way of expressing their emotions. Nor have they ever wallowed in self-pitying angst, preferring instead to turn their pain into something more positive. Bizarrely, this has been held against them. Linkin Park's confident, assured and original sound belied their tender years, and some refused to believe that a group still in their early twenties could have produced a first album so polished, innovative and well put together.

Basically, Linkin Park were too good to be true. The rumour started that they were a manufactured, boyband version of authentic nu-metal success stories like Limp Bizkit, Papa Roach and Korn, assembled by some unscrupulous record company. They were young and good-looking, and, some said, too squeaky clean. They didn't even have a Parental Advisory sticker on their CD cover. They must be fakes, right?

Certainly, Linkin Park have never deliberately courted controversy as a means to getting noticed, or indulged in the clichéd hero worship of serial killers like Charles Manson. They haven't advocated the use of drugs, firearms or pornography - although they haven't taken the moral high ground and condemned any of these things either. They have refused to sign female fans' naked breasts, and have repeatedly urged crowd members at large outdoor concerts not to sexually harass the girls in the audience. In this they're following in the footsteps of hardcore heroes like Nirvana, Henry Rollins and

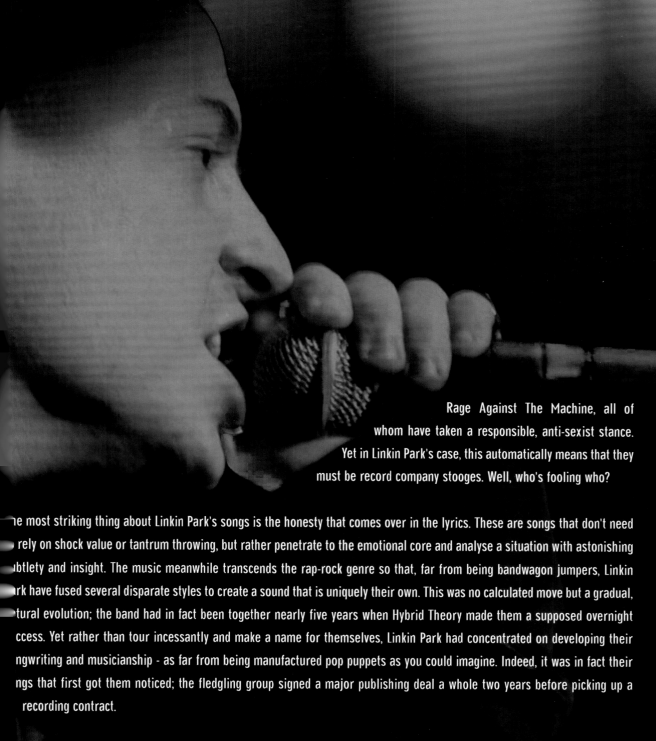

Rage Against The Machine, all of whom have taken a responsible, anti-sexist stance. Yet in Linkin Park's case, this automatically means that they must be record company stooges. Well, who's fooling who?

The most striking thing about Linkin Park's songs is the honesty that comes over in the lyrics. These are songs that don't need to rely on shock value or tantrum throwing, but rather penetrate to the emotional core and analyse a situation with astonishing subtlety and insight. The music meanwhile transcends the rap-rock genre so that, far from being bandwagon jumpers, Linkin Park have fused several disparate styles to create a sound that is uniquely their own. This was no calculated move but a gradual, natural evolution; the band had in fact been together nearly five years when Hybrid Theory made them a supposed overnight success. Yet rather than tour incessantly and make a name for themselves, Linkin Park had concentrated on developing their songwriting and musicianship - as far from being manufactured pop puppets as you could imagine. Indeed, it was in fact their songs that first got them noticed; the fledgling group signed a major publishing deal a whole two years before picking up a recording contract.

Linkin Park, then, are a band that invented themselves. A band whose success is down to nothing more sinister than the fact that they write great songs which sound fresh and go straight for the pop jugular. A band with lyrics that their audience can identify with, that are accessible yet give the listener something to think about. But don't be misled, the riffs and pounding beats still pump the moshpit full of adrenalin. Linkin Park are for real and their success story has only just begun.

The roots of Linkin Park go much deeper than you might imagine. As far back in fact as Junior High School in Agoura, Southern California, where a pre-teen Brad Delson and Mike Shinoda first became friends, discovered a shared passion for rap and rock music, and talked about forming a band.

By all accounts the pair were quiet, well-adjusted kids at school, popular among their peers while also being attentive to their studies. Neither belonged to any particular peer group; they weren't jocks or nerds, but individuals who found their identity through the music they listened to. The worst trouble that Mike ever got into at school was for trading "Garbage Pail Kids" cards in class, an activity that was only allowed during breaktimes. Luckily for the avid collector, the teacher didn't find his stash of cards and so he lived to swap again. Brad meanwhile actually got detention in eighth grade for talking out of turn, thus losing several hours that could have been spent practising on his beloved guitar. Needless to say, he made sure it didn't happen again.

An idea of Brad's family background can be gleaned from the fact that every year his parents hosted a charity Christmas dinner for local homeless people, and continue to do so to this day. Since childhood, Brad and Mike have helped out at the event, serving food and waiting on tables. As well as being a grounding experience and a lesson in responsibility, the pair always enjoyed the occasion and still look forward to it as the season comes around, helping out as much as Linkin Park's busy schedule allows.

While Brad was slowly learning to play the guitar, the half-Japanese Michael Kenji Shinoda was obsessed with art, computers and hip-hop. At this time, in the mid 1980s, the latter two were only just beginning to infringe on mainstream awareness, and few could predict the impact that they would have on our society. Yet early computer games, and the computer graphics that were still in their infancy, seemed somehow linked in many a schoolboy's mind with the crisp electro-beats, MC-ing, graffiti, breakdancing and body-popping culture that was, thanks to movies like *Wild Style*, then starting to spread across the globe.

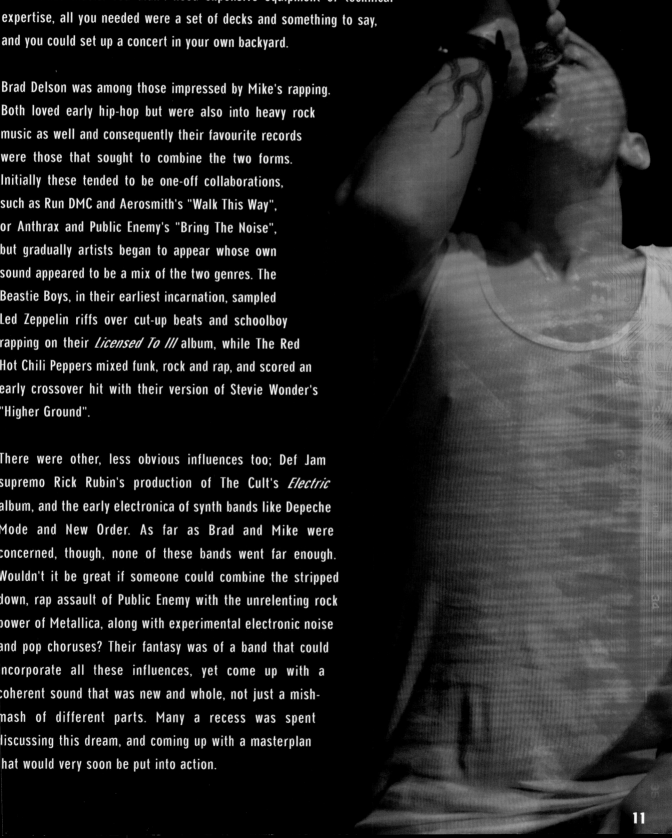

As well as copying out his favourite record sleeves and imitating graffiti tags in his artwork, Mike began rapping along with the likes of Run DMC, Eric B And Rakim, Grandmaster Flash and LL Cool J, trying to capture their lyrical flow and inspired, freestyling wordplay. He soon began inventing his own rhymes and would perform these for fun to his friends in the playground or after school. Hip-hop, like punk before it, seemed to suggest that anyone with a few good ideas and a bucketload of attitude could make music. You didn't need expensive equipment or technical expertise, all you needed were a set of decks and something to say, and you could set up a concert in your own backyard.

Brad Delson was among those impressed by Mike's rapping. Both loved early hip-hop but were also into heavy rock music as well and consequently their favourite records were those that sought to combine the two forms. Initially these tended to be one-off collaborations, such as Run DMC and Aerosmith's "Walk This Way", or Anthrax and Public Enemy's "Bring The Noise", but gradually artists began to appear whose own sound appeared to be a mix of the two genres. The Beastie Boys, in their earliest incarnation, sampled Led Zeppelin riffs over cut-up beats and schoolboy rapping on their *Licensed To Ill* album, while The Red Hot Chili Peppers mixed funk, rock and rap, and scored an early crossover hit with their version of Stevie Wonder's "Higher Ground".

There were other, less obvious influences too; Def Jam supremo Rick Rubin's production of The Cult's *Electric* album, and the early electronica of synth bands like Depeche Mode and New Order. As far as Brad and Mike were concerned, though, none of these bands went far enough. Wouldn't it be great if someone could combine the stripped down, rap assault of Public Enemy with the unrelenting rock power of Metallica, along with experimental electronic noise and pop choruses? Their fantasy was of a band that could incorporate all these influences, yet come up with a coherent sound that was new and whole, not just a mish-mash of different parts. Many a recess was spent discussing this dream, and coming up with a masterplan that would very soon be put into action.

After Junior High, Brad Delson was transferred to another high school, still in the North San Fernando Valley area of Southern California. It was here that the budding guitarist met Rob Bourdon who, as fate would have it, was just starting to play the drums. As the pair became friends, Brad told Rob about his other friend from junior high, Mike, and their still vague notion of forming a band that fused rock, rap, pop and electronica into a new musical style. Rob was immediately enthused by the idea. He was a die-hard funk fan, whose biggest influences were Earth, Wind And Fire and the James Brown band - anything in fact, with a funky beat. Rob and Brad began jamming together, while Mike frequently joined them to rap along over the top. The semblance of a genuine band was slowly starting to become a reality.

After high school, Mike Shinoda went on to study painting at the Pasadena Arts Centre, the most renowned college of its type in that part of the country. He soon hooked up with a fellow student, Joseph Hahn, who was also a massive hip-hop head. At this time though, hip-hop was still considered to be mostly the preserve of black, urban musicians, largely from America's east coast. The antics of watered-down pop acts like Vanilla Ice hadn't done much to improve the image of white rappers, yet Mike and Joe both saw no reason why there should be a colour bar on participating in this musical genre. Besides, with his mixed ancestry, Mike was hardly a typical middle class white boy attempting to muscle in on black territory. Having been brought up in two cultures himself, he automatically rebelled against any preconceived notions of ethnic groupings and exclusive musical purity. The whole point of rap, surely, was that anyone could do it, and that anything could be brought into the mix.

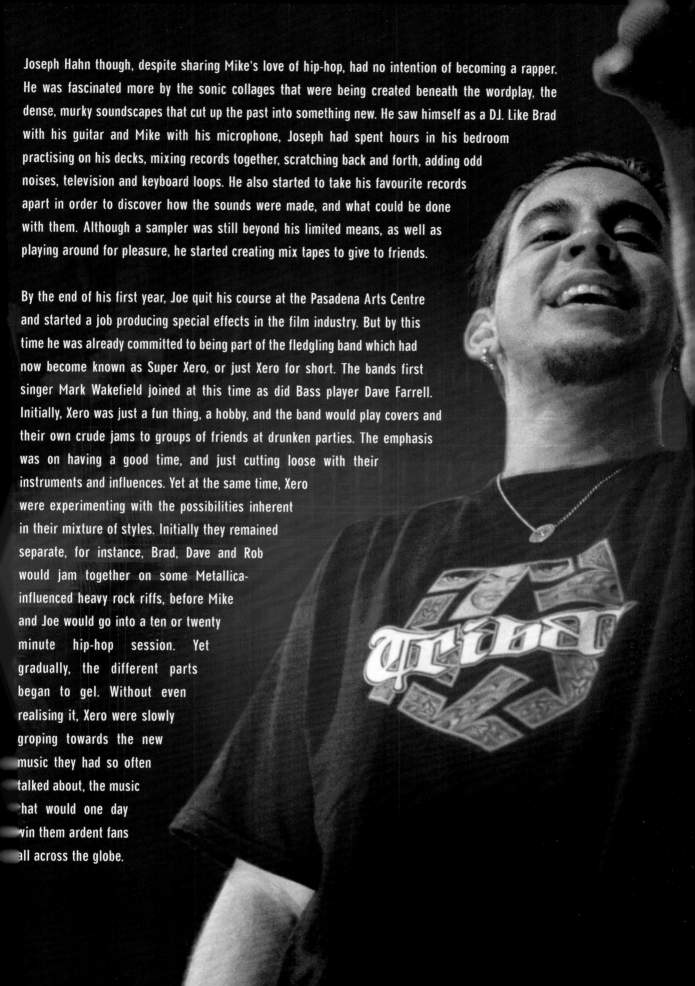

Joseph Hahn though, despite sharing Mike's love of hip-hop, had no intention of becoming a rapper. He was fascinated more by the sonic collages that were being created beneath the wordplay, the dense, murky soundscapes that cut up the past into something new. He saw himself as a DJ. Like Brad with his guitar and Mike with his microphone, Joseph had spent hours in his bedroom practising on his decks, mixing records together, scratching back and forth, adding odd noises, television and keyboard loops. He also started to take his favourite records apart in order to discover how the sounds were made, and what could be done with them. Although a sampler was still beyond his limited means, as well as playing around for pleasure, he started creating mix tapes to give to friends.

By the end of his first year, Joe quit his course at the Pasadena Arts Centre and started a job producing special effects in the film industry. But by this time he was already committed to being part of the fledgling band which had now become known as Super Xero, or just Xero for short. The bands first singer Mark Wakefield joined at this time as did Bass player Dave Farrell. Initially, Xero was just a fun thing, a hobby, and the band would play covers and their own crude jams to groups of friends at drunken parties. The emphasis was on having a good time, and just cutting loose with their instruments and influences. Yet at the same time, Xero were experimenting with the possibilities inherent in their mixture of styles. Initially they remained separate, for instance, Brad, Dave and Rob would jam together on some Metallica- influenced heavy rock riffs, before Mike and Joe would go into a ten or twenty minute hip-hop session. Yet gradually, the different parts began to gel. Without even realising it, Xero were slowly groping towards the new music they had so often talked about, the music that would one day win them ardent fans all across the globe.

As the nineties wore on, "Industrial" music came increasingly to the fore, and bands like Ministry, Nine Inch Nails and Front 242 would be added to the list of Xero's formative influences. Rage Against The Machine, too, were an important discovery for the young band, particularly for guitarist Tom Morello who would recreate the cut-up rhythms and scratching effects of a hip-hop DJ on his instrument, in between the fiercest of hardcore riffs.

While still essentially playing for fun, Xero did record a number of demo tapes, with Mark Wakefield singing, which they sent out to prospective booking agents and record companies. Among these was an early version of the song included on *Hybrid Theory* as "A Place For My Head", then titled "Esaul", and a check on the album's liner notes also reveals that Mark Wakefield gets songwriting credits on both "Forgotten" and "Runaway". Another song recorded by Xero that made it onto Linkin Park's debut album was "By Myself", which seems to capture the frustration and self-doubt the band were feeling at this stage of their career. No one was interested in the music they were making, and their families suggested that maybe it was time they all thought about getting proper jobs. The band too all wondered if they were wasting their time, but ultimately knew that they had no choice but to follow their instincts. As the song said, "If I'm killed by the questions like a cancer, then I'll be buried in the silence of the answer."

In the end, the band emerged from this period of uncertainty with a new resolve, and a new name; Hybrid Theory. Xero had been just for fun, for playing to their friends and messing around with different styles. Hybrid Theory reflected their intention to get serious as well as capturing a sense of the music they were attempting to create. This was essentially Mike and Brad's dream band from all those years ago, a group that could seamlessly fuse the best of rock and rap, pop and electronica. As Hybrid Theory concentrated on strengthening their songwriting, and realising their ambitions, required listening now included The Deftones, the schizophrenic soundscapes of The Aphex Twin, and the earthy hip-hop styling of The Roots and The Black Eyed Peas.

Eventually, their efforts paid off and Hybrid Theory secured a showcase gig at Los Angeles' famous Whisky club. Formerly named the Whisky-A-Go-Go, in the sixties this Sunset Strip bar had launched the careers of bands like The Doors and Jefferson Airplane. At this point, Brad was working as an intern at the top music publishing company Zomba Music and managed to convince his boss to come along and see his band play their first proper concert. Although the show was sparsely attended, Brad's boss was so impressed that he offered the band a publishing deal on the spot.

This breakthrough meant several things to the band. All right, it wasn't a record deal, but it was a foot in the door of the music industry. At Zomba they now had people who believed in them, and who would help them send out their songs to various contacts that might be able to help their career. Plus, it was a massive confidence boost to the band, a signal that someone else, a major professional organisation no less, believed in what they were doing, and in their ability to make it to the top. And there was also the small matter of a cash advance; not much, but enough for the band to set up a small home studio in Mike's room, with which they could work on new material.

The band continued to gig around the Los Angeles area, at one point playing a showcase for six record labels during the same weekend that Mike was sitting his finals at the Arts Centre in Pasadena. He later claimed he didn't sleep for two weeks from nervousness about this show. Despite this however, record companies just weren't biting, and doubts were once more starting to set in. Dave Farrell, was the first to jump ship, leaving the band to concentrate on work as a session musician. He would later return to the fold after the release of Linkin Park's debut album, but the sudden departure of singer Mark Wakefield was more permanent. The vocalist had never really gelled with the rest of the group, yet his going left an obvious gap that needed to be filled. Mike Shinoda was a perfectly competent frontman in his own right, yet to achieve the sound they were looking for the band really needed a traditional singer to compliment the rapper's biting lyrical skills. Zomba encouraged Hybrid Theory to work on honing their songwriting, while sending out instrumental demo tapes to prospective singers, requesting that they write and sing their own lyrics and melodies over the top. The search for the final part of the hybrid was on.

CHAPTER 4 THE FIFTH ELEMENT

Chester Bennington was born in Phoenix, Arizona on the twentieth of March 1976. At school he was a self-confessed "nerd" who didn't fit in anywhere, until he discovered music. A hyperactive, extroverted kid, he claims that from the age of two he was running around mimicking songs he'd heard on the radio, telling everyone that he was going to be a singer. His parents divorced when he was eleven, and by the time he was in his early teens, Chester was addicted to both cocaine and methamphetamine. "I went straight in the wrong direction," he later commented, and admits that the anger he felt then, and the situations he experienced, definitely fuelled the intensity that radiates from him on stage.

Chester's first taste of performing was actually as a child actor and he had an early taste of touring while travelling around the country appearing in various theatrical productions. He had already seen most of the states of the union by the age of fourteen when he made his live debut as a singer. By the time he was recommended to Hybrid Theory, Chester had been performing solo or with various bands for almost nine years, and had even released an album with a group called Grey Daze, entitled *No Sun Today*. His formative musical influences were found within his older brother's collection of eighties soft rock - Rush, Loverboy and, especially, Foreigner, whose impact is still apparent in Linkin Park's anthemic choruses. Later on, his singing style was moulded by listening to Scott Weiland of Stone Temple Pilots and Al Jourgensen of Ministry. Quitting drugs, falling in love and getting married all by the age of twenty, Chester seemed to have lived several lives by the time his lawyer, of all people, told him that there was this great new band out in Los Angeles that were looking for a singer.

By chance, Hybrid Theory and Chester Bennington shared the same law firm, Miniet, Phelps and Phelps. They astutely realised that they handled both a band that were looking for a singer and a singer that was looking for a band, and put the two parties in contact with each other. Chester was so inspired by Hybrid Theory's instrumental demo tape that he actually missed his own twenty-third birthday party in order to write and record his vocals over it. Just a few days after Hybrid Theory had sent out the tape, a breathless Chester rang them back to say he'd just finished adding his parts. "What, already?" they wondered, before asking him to play back some of the tape down the phone, which he did. Three days later, Chester was flying out to LA, leaving everything behind him to join the band. His wife followed him a month or so later.

With Chester on board, people slowly began to pay attention. The singer's mammoth, anthemic vocal style clicked immediately with Mike Shinoda's streetwise rapping, and the band soon realised that their new sound now had massive commercial possibilities. Accordingly, they continued to work on their songwriting, making the lyrics and tunes more accessible, more powerful and straightforward. There was no point in being obscure for the sake of it, they felt. Why not try to reach as many people as possible?

Linkin Park are now considered to be one of the first generation of bands to have grown up on the Internet, and this can be put down to Mike and Rob's early interest in the possibilities of computer technology. Both immediately saw the potential inherent in the 'net for publicising the band, and while unsigned they worked hard on designing their own website. This enabled them to reach fans not only across the USA, but also globally. Hybrid Theory, though, went one step further than most. They specifically set out to use the Internet as a way to involve their fans directly in the process of promoting the group. Through the World-Wide Web they recruited "Street Teams" in various corners of the United States, each one co-ordinated by a "Captain" who would receive demo tapes, posters, stickers and badges to distribute around their local neighbourhood. When the band came to play a gig in that particular town, the local Street Team would be involved from the outset, helping to promote the concert and so on.

In a sense, the Street Teams were a cross between the grass-roots network that has supported the punk and hardcore scene since the early eighties, and some kind of pre-war, Boy Scout newspaper drive. It was the idea of the Internet as a virtual community taken at its word, allowing isolated pockets of fans to feel a part of the growing success of the band, a mutual relationship that benefited both parties. Later on, Linkin Park always acknowledged the importance of the Internet, and the Street Teams, in aiding their success.

With Chester now an integral part of the band, Hybrid Theory felt confident enough to release two, three-track EPs of new material with lyrics co-written by Mike and Chester. Mainly intended to be sent out to contacts within the industry during 1998, these six songs already capture the raw potential that would reach full fruition on Linkin Park's debut album. The likes of "Step Up" and "Carousel" display both anger and sensitivity, while the hip-hop track, "High Voltage", appeared in remixed form on the b-side of Linkin Park's first single, *One Step Closer*. Like their early demos, the EPs were written and recorded on the portastudio in Mike's house on Stocker Street, where the paper thin walls did little to contain the sound of the group playing at full blast. They would later recount how, at exactly ten PM each night, the neighbours would bang loudly on the walls, like an alarm call, signalling that they should stop playing for the night. In fact, the band nearly called themselves Ten PM Stocker because of this.

Despite the displeasure of Mike's neighbours, however, Hybrid Theory's live shows were steadily starting to build up a buzz around the LA scene. When an Internet promotional company called Streetwise Concepts And Culture put a song called "Plaster" - an early version of "One Step Closer" - on their website, the band suddenly started to receive serious interest. With Chester's show-stopping vocals and intense stage presence, it was inevitable that Linkin Park would eventually secure a major label contract and, in 1999, they finally signed on the dotted line with Warner Brothers. The Hybrid was now complete.

With the higher profile that comes from being signed to a major record company, Hybrid Theory soon ran into trouble. They discovered that several other bands existed with names similar to theirs, and were warned that there could be various unpleasant legal difficulties if they continued to trade under their current name. To avoid this the band decided it would be easier to simply change their name, and began casting around for an alternative suggestion. Numerous options were considered, including Clear and, if some stories are to be believed, Probing Lagers and Platinum Lotus Foundation. The eventual answer though, as in so many Hollywood movies, was to be found right in their own backyard.

Chester was by now living in the Santa Monica area of Los Angeles, near a park by the name of Lincoln. Lincoln Park. "Hey that would be a cool name for a band," Chester thought, and suggested it to the rest of the group. Without any of them realising it, something about the name connected to the energy of the band, and it just began to feel right. So Hybrid Theory became Lincoln Park, and set out on a nation-wide tour of the country under that name; only to find that almost every town they went to had a park called Lincoln, and every town assumed that they must be a local band, named after their own particular patch of green. For a while this became a band in-joke, that they were a local group wherever they went. More seriously though, with Lincoln Park being such a common place name, and one which featured the name of one of America's best-loved presidents, the band found that the Internet domain name would be practically impossible to secure. So, they changed the spelling, dropping the C-O-L from Lincoln and adding a K and an I, creating an identity which, like their music, was familiar, memorable and yet entirely their own.

It was as Linkin Park that the band released their debut album, *Hybrid Theory*, on October 24th 2000. Featuring twelve killer tracks, yet clocking in at less than thirty-eight minutes, the record rocketed straight into the Billboard album charts at number sixteen, an unprecedented achievement for a previously unknown band. Linkin Park's use of the Internet, and the loyalty and devotion of their Street Teams, obviously contributed to the CD's success, but most important of all was the fact that the album contained a collection of great tunes. All that dedication to craft and songwriting had finally paid off.

The band admitted that they had made some lyrical and structural changes for the LP. Songs were made more accessible and metaphors more straightforward, emphasising the raw honesty and emotion at their core. Linkin Park always intended that their songs should reach out and communicate with people, saying something to them about their lives. The band all collaborate on songwriting, and without exception are aware of how to develop a song and bring out its strengths. Lyrically, on songs like "One Step Closer", "A Place For My Head", or "In The End", the band will usually start with a personal situation and then develop the theme so that it becomes universal, and could apply to anyone.

Hybrid Theory is an astonishing debut, one that manages to sound both confident and troubled, well-produced yet raw, melodic yet harsh and confrontational. The band themselves claimed that the phrase "Hybrid Theory" now meant more to them than simply a mix of rock and rap music, but rather a broader combination of rage and melancholy, frustration and positivity, darkness and light. Linkin Park believe that the opening track, "Papercut" is the one that best represents them, capturing their fluid fusion of beats, guitars, rapping and strong pop vocals, with personal, introspective lyrics that set the tone for the whole album. They also say that their concentration on composition and songwriting is what separates them from other rap-rock bands; the fact that they're more likely to look inwards than out, that they concentrate on the emotion rather than the response. "We're not really a kick-your-ass type of band," they say.

One *Step Closer* with its frustrated, catchy refrain of "Shut up when I'm talking to you," was the album's first single, and was accompanied by a striking video directed by Gregory Dark. Dark was chosen by Joe Hahn, who also came up with the concept for the video, following his years of work in the movie industry. Filmed in an abandoned subway tunnel in LA, adjacent to a derelict veteran's hospital, the band claim that the shoot was frightening and difficult. The air was thick with dust and dirt, making it almost impossible to breathe, which succeeded in creating the atmosphere they'd hoped for perfectly.

Legendary hip-hop producers The Dust Brothers, best known for their work with Beck, were brought in to contribute to the third track, "With You". The collaboration came about when the Brothers sent Linkin Park a tape of drum loops and different synth and moog sounds, over which Linkin Park added guitars, live drums and vocals. The result is one of the album's standout tracks, with a dark, nightmarish lyric characterised by obsession and regret. Elsewhere, "Crawling" is one of the album's most immediately accessible tracks, resembling a pumped-up Depeche Mode, while the Metallica-ish "In The End" is a gloom-rock anthem that has become a strong live favourite. Both songs showcase Brad Delson's innovative use of harmonics in his guitar playing. What often sounds like walls of atmospheric synthesiser is in fact just Brad's guitar, switching styles with the expertise of a true craftsman. Mister Hahn, meanwhile, gets to show off his DJ skills on the trip-hop instrumental, "Cure For The Itch", before the CD ends with the final, epic crescendo of "Pushing Me Away".

Pearl Jam's producer Don Gilmore, had been chosen by the band to work with them from a list of several candidates, because they knew that he would push them to work harder. And push them he did, so much so that *Hybrid Theory* quickly started selling in massive amounts. Despite being released in the run-up to Christmas. Linkin Park were suddenly thrust into the spotlight, and soon found themselves being treated like The New Kids On The Block in more ways

CHAPTER 6 OVERNIGHT SUCCESS?

It's hard to believe now, but initially the music business just didn't understand Linkin Park. Sure, the rap-rock crossover was all the rage, but as far as some record companies were concerned, Linkin Park just weren't doing it the way it was meant to be done. They weren't a party band like Limp Bizkit or Kid Rock, but were tapping into a darker, more intellectual strain of hip-hop that was influenced by the likes of Mos Def, Common, The Roots and The Black Eyed Peas. But the music biz assumed that there was only one way to do the rap-rock crossover, and kept on at the band to change their style if they wanted to get signed. Thankfully, Linkin Park stuck to their guns and were rewarded with an album that sold nearly three-hundred-thousand copies in its first month of release.

Linkin Park were fast becoming a success story that no one had expected to happen. They seemed literally to have come out of nowhere, yet of course, this was hardly the case. Five years in the making, their hybrid of hip-hop, heavy metal, pop and electronica wasn't a contrived, calculated combination of popular styles, it was the inevitable result of growing up listening to different kinds of music. Linkin Park's goal was always to create a record where there was no separation between the rock, rap and whatever other elements they might inject into the mix, a record where they all just gelled naturally, and in this they succeeded. By the time *Hybrid Theory* was released, this was no big deal to them, it was just the way that modern music was sounding.

In a way, Linkin Park's timing couldn't have been better. The moment was exactly right for the sound that they'd been honing for all those years, but for some it seemed a little too right. The same voices in the industry that had previously told Linkin Park that they were doing it all wrong now accused them of jumping on the rap-rock bandwagon, of cynically manufacturing the ultimate crossover album, or worse, of being actually manufactured themselves. By lacing nu-metal's downtuned riffs and angry rapping with sugar sweet melodies and pop choruses, some considered that Linkin Park were selling out the genre, heading straight for the mainstream and winning over the little kids weaned on N-Sync and The Backstreet Boys, as well as their older brothers and sisters.

Of course, any unprejudiced listen to *Hybrid Theory*, and a glance through its lyric sheet, will tell you that these accusations are untrue. Here are a band as powerful and real as any, and who sound nothing like the credible bands they're supposedly ripping off. Linkin Park are clearly true originals, whose sound is rooted in old-school innovators like Rage Against The Machine, Metallica and Depeche Mode, not the current sounds they would be aping if they really were a cynically manufactured cash-in. Plus, there are the lyrics that bleed with raw honesty and poetic intelligence, their ferocity remaining undiminished by the inventive melody lines that Chester and the band come up with around them.

Nevertheless, following the unprecedented success of *Hybrid Theory*, the rumour began to spread that Linkin Park were actually put together by pop svengali Lou Pearlman. The argument was that they were too slick too seamless, that they'd had it too easy. To top it all off, they didn't even swear on their album. Each member o Linkin Park seemed to resemble the token "rebel" that every manufactured boyband has to have these days, with the pierced eyebrow, dreadlocks and discreet tattoos. The rumour was entirely unfounded, of course, but it stuck, much to the band's annoyance. They never heard the story themselves until they left the US and began touring Europe where they told journalists that they were thinking of adding a "Bash A Boy Band" game to their website.

The simple fact remains that Linkin Park are the band that the record companies wish they'd manufactured. Their huge popularity can simply be put down to them being one of the hardest working bands in the business and because they're good at what they do. They connect with people, finding the common ground between the wildest freaks, sensitive, introverted kids, suburban jocks and streetwise b-boys. Anyone who doesn't believe the hype knows that Linkin Park are as real as it gets.

More serious, perhaps, than accusations that Linkin Park were fakes, were the accusations that they were too real. Or to be more precise, that their lyrics and music encouraged their fans to act on their darkest feelings and frustrations, often with violent and tragic consequences.

On March the fifth 2001, nearly six months after the release of *Hybrid Theory*, a fifteen-year-old schoolboy named Charles Andrew Williams but known as Andy after the middle of the road ballad singer Andy Williams, packed a gun in his bag as he set off for school. Later that day, at Santana High School in the small town of Santee, near San Diego in California, he opened fire on his classmates, killing two and injuring thirteen. No one could work out a reason for this seemingly unprovoked attack, one of a string of such incidents in American high schools in recent years. But, as in many similar cases, and with equally shaky reasoning, the media decided to put the blame on the music that the killer was listening to. In Charles Williams' case, that music was Linkin Park.

Friends of the troubled teenager told U.S. TV's *Today* show that Charles Williams' favourite band was Linkin Park, and that he listened to their album almost religiously. His favourite tracks were "To The End", "Papercut" and "One Step Closer", from which the show's host solemnly read the lyric, "Cause I'm one step closer to the edge, and I'm about to break." From then on, this supposed connection to Linkin Park was widely reported in the media, and right-wing pundits and politicians (the same ones who campaign against gun control) shouted that rock music had claimed yet more victims.

To their credit, Linkin Park handled the situation with dignity and maturity, while distancing themselves from any suggestion of responsibility. "Like everyone else, we are extremely saddened by these events and our hearts go out to the families and friends of the victims," said their official statement. They later pointed out to interviewers that the type of music a killer listens to has nothing to do with the reasoning behind their actions, any more than the type of socks he wears. He may share that choice with a student class president, a judge or a policeman's son, and probably even some of his victims. "You might as well say, it's because he ate mayonnaise that day," Chester commented.

It's no surprise that someone with deep rooted feelings of anger and resentment should find something to identify with in Linkin Park's music, just as, for example, John Lennon's killer Mark Chapman identified with JD Salinger's classic novel *The Catcher In The Rye*. But it's worth remembering that most serial killers' preferred choice of reading is *The Bible*. Great works of art often connect with our most buried feelings, and those who feel isolated and alone are bound to make connections on a deeper level than others. Yet, as Brad points out, "Those emotions are the things we write about. But to take the leap from those emotions to something violent is nothing to do with us."

Nevertheless, rock groups continue to be demonised for problems that in fact go right to the heart of American society. Just as Marilyn Manson was widely held to be responsible for the bloodshed at Columbine, despite later revelations that the killers actually hated his music, so Linkin Park are told that because they offer a positive outlet for the anger and frustration that everyone feels, they are to blame when one unstable teenager cracks under the pressure of modern life. "There's not enough attention paid to the problems of sensitive young men in our society," Chester has mused, and if anything, Linkin

CHAPTER 8 REACHING OUT

For Linkin Park, as for so many other rock groups, success has meant going out on the road. Although they didn't tour much in their early days, preferring to concentrate on writing and recording, since signing to Warner Brothers in 1999 they've been playing live almost constantly, honing their craft and connecting every night with those who've always mattered most to them - their fans.

Linkin Park are known, more than anything else, for their dedication to their followers. Apart from their Internet Street Teams, another reason for the immediate success of *Hybrid Theory* was that prior to its release the band would hang out after their shows for several hours in the freezing cold, meeting fans, signing t-shirts and chatting, until the venue was empty and everyone had gone home. Even well after the album's release, when they felt like they'd been on the road forever, Linkin Park continued to get excited about meeting their hardcore fans. For Chester in particular, the band's success has confirmed his belief that people everywhere do have some common ground, and he feels honoured that Linkin Park have managed to connect so deeply with so many different people.

Constant touring does have its drawbacks, however. The band only recently graduated to a tourbus, having spent many months with nine people, plus equipment, crammed into a six berth camper van, driving from one gig to another without sleep, learning to live with the smell of each other's stale laundry. Sleep is still a luxury, particularly when playing overseas, as Linkin Park get no chance to recover from jet lag, or adjust to time differences. A typical day may involve up to thirty interviews and half a dozen photo shoots before the main business of the concert in the evening, then travelling overnight to the next date on the tour. So they're up all night, every night, and most of each day, surviving on the odd catnap that revives them for an hour or two but leaves them more tired than they were before. Plus there is the strain of being separated from family and loved ones. Chester admits that he had to phone up his wife from on tour just to be reminded of what his home address was.

Nevertheless, Linkin Park love touring, and feel eternally grateful for being given the chance to do what they love for a living. While they enjoy the life, they know its pitfalls, and understand the strict standards they have to maintain to get through it in one piece. As a result, there is a no smoking or drinking rule on Linkin Park's tourbus, and no alcohol on their tour riders. If someone wants to get drunk they can do it at a club after the show, but for Linkin Park playing is their job. If they're wasted they feel they're not doing that job properly. They have a responsibility, to their fans, their families and the people working for them, and they take that responsibility seriously. Instead of boozing, they while away the hours on the bus gambling, playing poker and blackjack with the road crew.

For Chester, the highlight of the year 2000 was meeting his hero, Scott Weiland of Stone Temple pilots, backstage momentarily at a festival that both bands were playing. Although they only spoke for a couple of seconds and Chester fumbled his words, not knowing what to say, he came away overjoyed and tremendously excited. Even though his own band has now encountered huge success, Chester Bennington remains a fan, and one who claims he doesn't yet feel famous himself. Despite this, Linkin Park have

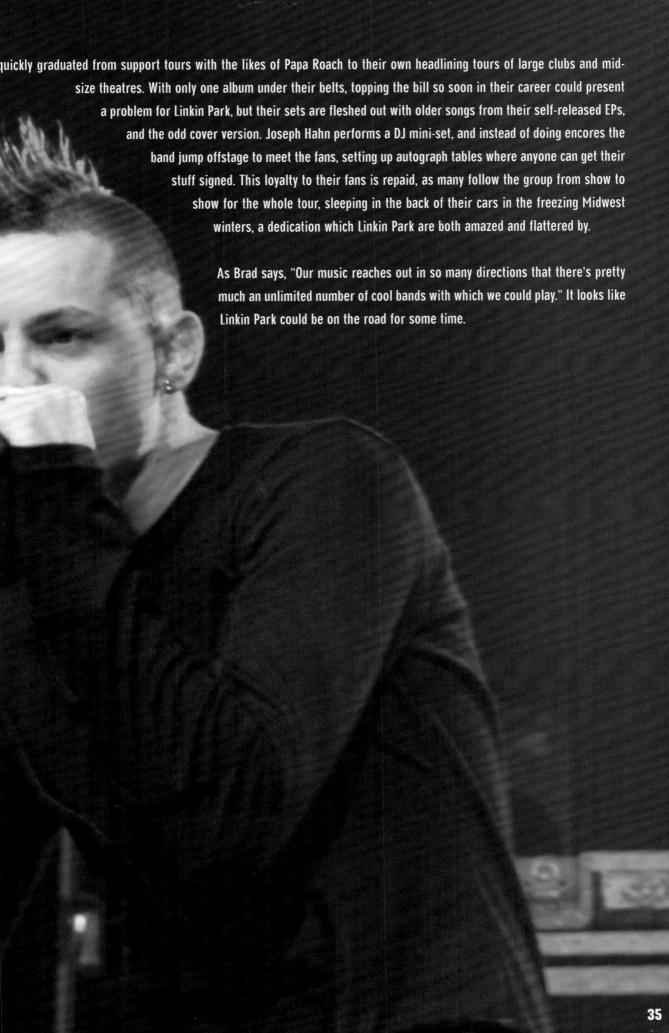

quickly graduated from support tours with the likes of Papa Roach to their own headlining tours of large clubs and mid-size theatres. With only one album under their belts, topping the bill so soon in their career could present a problem for Linkin Park, but their sets are fleshed out with older songs from their self-released EPs, and the odd cover version. Joseph Hahn performs a DJ mini-set, and instead of doing encores the band jump offstage to meet the fans, setting up autograph tables where anyone can get their stuff signed. This loyalty to their fans is repaid, as many follow the group from show to show for the whole tour, sleeping in the back of their cars in the freezing Midwest winters, a dedication which Linkin Park are both amazed and flattered by.

As Brad says, "Our music reaches out in so many directions that there's pretty much an unlimited number of cool bands with which we could play." It looks like Linkin Park could be on the road for some time.

In the summer of 2001 Linkin Park set out on the Ozzfest tour, the legendary metal roadshow across America, headlined by Ozzy Osbourne and Black Sabbath. Also on the bill were Mudvayne, Disturbed, Papa Roach and Slipknot, with whom Linkin Park played a handful of "Off Fest" shows between scheduled dates. Also, in 2001 the band made guest appearances on several other records, including the X-ecutioners LP *Built From Scratch*, which also featured the likes of Xzibit, Pharaoh Monch, Inspectah Deck and so on. In addition, Chester sang on the track "Karma Killer" on Cyclefly's *Tales From The Fishbowl* LP, while the band had songs on the soundtrack albums to the films *Dracula 2000*, *Valentine* and *Little Nicky*.

With only one album under their belts, Linkin Park are already the equals of nu-metal titans like Papa Roach and Korn. Their attention to detail and traditional songwriting values have catapulted them directly into the mainstream, yet they've never sacrificed the authentic rage and ferocity that has fuelled them from the start. Many are surprised at how approachable Linkin Park are as people, but they claim that they've never wanted to alienate anyone. Unlike some bands who go to great lengths to emphasise how weird they are, Linkin Park always try to come over as regular guys. As Chester says, there's no cape and leotard under his clothes, what you see is what you get. Even his openness about his past life and drug problems are not to show off his suffering as a badge of credibility, but to say to others, if I've come through it, you can too.

From the start, Linkin Park's music has carried a positive message. Although their songs are about the doubts and frustrations of everyday life, the darkness that everybody holds within them, they never offer the easy option of withdrawal into self-destructive behaviour, or lashing out violently against others. Neither though, would they ever write a dumb party anthem, pretending that everything's OK once you've got money, girls, and success. Linkin Park are about recognising the pain and paranoia within, and dealing with it. They express this in the only way they know how - through words and music.

Still all in their early twenties, Linkin Park are a band that can identify with their audience because they are their audience; young people trying to grow up in the new millennium, dealing with all the issues of the modern world.

They aren't thirty-somethings trying desperately to write songs that "the kids" can identify with. In fact, Linkin Park are still going through growing pains themselves, trying to reconcile the idealism and helplessness of youth with the responsibilities, compromises and hypocrisies of adult life. The paranoia and self-doubt evident in "Papercut" is from the heart, as is the rage and resentment of "Points Of Authority" or the existential despair of "In The End". Linkin Park still mean it, and success certainly hasn't washed their feelings of insecurity away.

Six thoughtful, sensitive, and deeply spiritual individuals, Linkin Park care enough about their music to be making it for a long time yet. One step closer to the edge, their strength is in their vulnerability, and their desire to keep on reaching out to the world. If we continue caring for as long as they do, then Linkin Park could well be around forever.

"We support free music.
So go ahead! Download that shit!" Mike

"In this country, people do not think about the sensitivity of young men. It's a real tragedy. For kids to be able to listen to bands like us who are able to express ourselves - not through violence and vulgarity - I think it helps them learn to express themselves." Chester

"We're not a bunch of goody-two-shoes, but we do have responsibilities to ourselves and our families and the people in this group, and we respect that." Chester

"Come to the shows, come and meet us, because we love to hang out, every time we have a show we will come to our merchandise booth and we will meet all of you and talk and sign autographs or whatever, just come out." Mike

"Our Lincoln Park is in Santa Monica, CA. But when we started national touring, everyone thought we were a local band wherever we went, because there are so many Lincoln Parks everywhere. It was basically our band joke: we were local everywhere we went." Mike

"We try to meet as many fans as possible. If we could meet everyone at the venue, that would be great, but sometimes it's impossible. I hope that they walk away thoroughly enjoying the band. And just become fans and enjoy the music that we make."

"We're not very photogenic!" Brad

"I always wanted to be a rock star. That was my childhood dream. That's what I told everybody I was going to be when I grew up." Chester

"We know who we are and we're not going to change that." Chester

"I think, in the lyrics, we're generally a little more introverted, a little more just trying to be honest and sum up some of these everyday universal emotions that we all feel. And that is something that's, hopefully, just as individual as the way each person talks." Mike

"We go for raw emotions, not just some story about a social situation. We mainly focus on laying out an emotional starting point from which the listener can begin relating their own story." Chester

"We're not a bunch of goody-two-shoes, but we do have responsibilities to ourselves and our families and the people in this group, and we respect that." Chester

"We've been hit and broken things. Brad's guitar has hit me in the head before. I actually threw up in my mouth in Des Moines." Mike

"If I weren't passionate about this, I'd do something else I was passionate about. We hope a lot of people will get something out of the music we're making. That's why we're in a band - it's communication." Brad

"My favourite jellybean is the pink one with the flavour inside." Chester

"We're pretty straight guys: we're not boozers, we're not fucked up on drugs." Chester

"I'm just a regular guy, you know? There's no leotard and cape under my clothes. I shit, I piss, I drink too much and throw up, just like everybody else." Chester

"I think that it's a melting pot where we've got a lot of things that come together but in the end they all just gel and just become one song and that's what is most important to us. It's just a song. It's not the rap part and the rock part and the electronic part and the singing part and the rapping and the screaming and the whispering." Mike

"We're shooting for the title of hardest-working band in America." Chester

"It has never been our goal to be like popular, if you ask different people in the band they will have different answers, but my goal was to blend the different types of music, and not to say, this is going to be the hip hop part and this is going to be the rock part, we want you to hear our songs and know that your listening to Linkin Park." Mike

"We write a lot of the songs together. The choruses are so important for example that everybody has a little bit of a say in what goes on. You never hurt anybody's feelings by talking about any parts of the songs. Everybody has their say and writes the songs and we're all really proud of what we've come up with." Mike

"We want to give people a starting block with the lyrics so that they can relate their own story to it. Our songs come from something that happened to us or an emotion that we feel. We want it put it out there in a way that is as accurate to the way we feel as we can say it." Mike

"We just want to be honest and not hide any emotions with vulgarity." Chester

"There's wacky girls all over the place that try doing weird things, but we don't pay attention to them. We just kind of do our thing and hang out with the fans that are really important to us." Chester

"I always wanted to be a rock star. That was my childhood dream. That's what I told everybody I was going to be when I grew up." Chester

"We are making our way to actually becoming a boy band. Our first video is gonna have all of us in a shower wearing white linen suits, crying and pointing at the camera. We definitely want to start wearing matching outfits, choreographing, and lip-syncing our live show." Mike

I chew my fingernails a lot, I think that's my little nervous habit. That's one of my ways to relieve stress. If you see me chew my nails, I'm probably nervous about something." Chester

41

CHAPTER 11 DISCOGRAPHY

ALBUMS AND E.P.'s

Hybrid Theory EP
Carousel / Technique / Step Up / And One / High Voltage / Part Of Me

CD - Warner 2000

Hybrid Theory
Papercut / One Step Closer / With You / Points Of Authority / Crawling / Runaway / By Myself / In the End / A Place for My Head / Forgotten / Cure for the Itch / Pushing Me Away

CD - Warner 2000

Hybrid Theory
Papercut / One Step Closer / With You / Points Of Authority / Crawling / Runaway / By Myself / In The End / A Place For My Head / Forgotten / Cure For The Itch / Pushing Me Away / My December / High Voltage - Japanese version featuring 2 bonus tracks: *My December* and *High Voltage.*

CD - Warner 2001

SINGLES

One Step Closer
One Step Closer (Album Version) / One Step Closer (Rock Mix)

CD - Warner 2001

One Step Closer
One Step Closer / With You / Points of Authority

CD - Warner 2001

One Step Closer
One Step Closer / High Voltage / My December

CD - Warner 2001

One Step Closer
One Step Closer / My December / High Voltage (Remix) / One Step Closer (CD-Rom Video)

CD - Warner 2001

Crawling
Crawling (Album Version) / Papercut (Live From The BBC) / Backstage Video Footage (Enhanced CD-Rom Video)

CD - Warner 2001

Paper Cut
Papercut / Points Of Authority (Live Radio One Session From London Docklands Arena) / Papercut (Live Radio One Session From London Docklands Arena) / Papercut (CD-Rom Video)

CD - Warner 2001

In the End
In the End

CD - Warner 2001

ALBUMS WITH OTHER ARTISTS / COMPILATIONS

MTV's Return of the Rock Vol. 2
One Step Closer

CD - Roadrunner 2000

KROQ Christmas Compilation
My December

CD - BMG/Time Bomb Recordings 2000

Ozzfest 2001: Second Millennium
With You

CD - Sony/Epic 2001

Built From Scratch
It's Going Down - The X-ecutioners with Linkin Park on guitar and vocals

CD - Loud Records 2001

Greetings From Santa Monica
Karma Killer - Promo CD sampler for Cyclefly's forthcoming album "Tales From The Fishbowl". Featuring Chester Bennington on vocals.

CD - Universal/Radioactive 2001

LINKIN PARK

CRAWLING

ENHANCED CD INCLUDING

FOOTAGE

LINKIN PARK

[HYBRID THEORY]

LINKIN PARK

ONE STEP CLOSER

1: *Album Version* 2:36
2: *Rock Mix* 2:36

SOUNDTRACKS

Dracula 2000 Soundtrack

One Step Closer

CD - Sony/Columbia 2000

Little Nicky Soundtrack

Points Of Authority

CD - WEA/Warner Brothers 2000

Valentine Soundtrack

Pushing Me Away

CD - WEA/Warner Brothers 2001

BOOKS AND AUDIO BOOKS

Linkin Park

The Unauthorised Biography in Words and Pictures

Chrome Dreams 2001

Maximum Linkin Park

Audio-Biography

CD - Chrome Dreams 2001

Hybrid Theory

Songbook With Music and Lyrics From The Album Hybrid Theory

Warner Brother's Publications 2001

DVD

Crawling

Crawling (Live Video Version) / Crawling (Album Version Audio) / Be Myself, With You, One Step Closer and A Place For My Head (4 x 30 Second Live Video Snippets)

DVD - Warner 2001

BOOTLEGS

Bootlegs are unofficial releases of mixes, live recordings, downloads and rare tracks. There are numerous such items around featuring Linkin Park and below are a selection of the most common ones. It should be noted that to sell or trade in bootleg material is a criminal offence, therefore they are only available from underground sources such as market stalls and record fairs. The authors and publishers of the book do not endorse any trade in such items nor do they have any further information about their availability.

Orlando 2000

Papercut / Forgotten / Points of Authority / With You / Runaway / And One / In The End / A Place For My Head / One Step Closer

Rock AM Ring

With You / Runaway / Papercut / By Myself / Points Of Authority / High Voltage / Crawling / Pushing Me Away / And One / In The End / A Place For My Head / Cure For The Itch / One Step Closer

Roseland Ballroom New York, NY 11.10.00

A Place For My Head / Forgotten / Papercut / By Myself / In The End /With You / One Step Closer

Roseland Ballroom New York, NY 02.21.01

With You / Runaway / Papercut / By Myself / Points of Authority / High Voltage (Remix) / Crawling / Pushing Me Away / And One /In the End / A Place for My Head / Forgotten /One Step Closer

Ozzfest 2001 Chicago, Tinley Park 06.08.01

A Place For My Head / Forgotten / Papercut / Points Of Authority / By Myself / In The End / Crawling / With You / Runaway / One Step Closer

For sourcing additional information about Linkin Park, you really can't beat the World Wide Web. There are numerous sites about the band containing a wide range of biographical information, pictures, up-to-the-minute news and tour dates as well as MP3s of both their well known and rarer tracks. The following sites are among the most comprehensive and a good place to start finding out about Linkin Park online. Search engines such as Yahoo and Google can uncover many more fan sites. Up-to-date information can also be found on general music sites such as www. rollingstone.com, www.nme.com, www.mtv.com and www.getmusic.com.

www.linkinpark.com

This official record company site should be your first port of call. There is a great flash introduction so don't be tempted just to skip past it. The most recent band news is conveniently placed on the front page from where you can navigate to lyrics, MP3s and videos of tracks from *Hybrid Theory*. There is also stacks of tour information as well as details of past and future gigs and an official band biography. The lack of photos is more than made up for by the Linkin Park message board and online chat section. You can also check out useful guitar and bass tablature for tracks from the album and purchase a range of Linkin Park merchandise on-line from shirts, t-shirts, jackets and Hoodies to bumper stickers.

www.linkinparkweb.com

Tom Mattson who runs this site has done a great job. There is a comprehensive Linkin Park news section that is even more comprehensive than that on the official site! There is also a large music section with Real Audio versions of pretty much every recorded Linkin Park track (including tracks off the *Hybrid Theory EP*) plus lyrics, guitar and bass tablature. The site is littered with tons of photos and includes a biography section as well as an area where fans can upload and exhibit their Linkin Park inspired art. A full press section containing text of articles about the band and transcriptions of interviews, a multimedia section, message board and the promise of future competitions round off one of the best Linkin Park sites around.

www.linkinpark-network.com

Another comprehensive Linkin Park site. The current and breaking news area on the right hand side also includes their current chart positions. The front page also includes a poll that you can enter as well as links to lyrics, tablature, a biography and discography. There is also a really useful Linkin Park FAQ answering such questions as the age of the members, how to contact them and when their next album will be released. You can also find tour information, articles on the band, interviews, audio and video as well as a number of photos. At the site's interactive area you can sign the guest book, post a message on the forum, check out fan art as well as concert and album reviews. The advertising pop-up pages, though, are somewhat annoying.

www.linkin-park.com

The homepage of the Linkin Park Underground. The usual individual biographies and band history, plus an in depth miscellaneous information section which contains tons of interesting facts from Pheonix's favourite sports to Chester's ideal night out. From here you can also buy Linkin Park CDs at CD-Now as well as check out MP3 versions of all their tracks. The download section includes several Linkin Park calenders as well as pictures and wallpaper files that you can download and use on your computer's desktop. In the midst of the usual guestbooks, polls and message boards you can also find a quiz where you can test your knowledge about Linkin Park.

Other Web Sites

www.hybrid-theory.com
www.guiltylinkin.cjb.net
www.linkinparkmusic.net
www.angelfire.com/band/linkinpk/
www.lpark.homestead.com/
www.pushmeaway.com
www.lpfan.com
www.linkinparkcentral.com

linkinparkfan@hotmail.com - Send an email here to subscribe to the Linkin Park "Inside" mailing list which is run by Chester's brother, Brian Bennington.

PHOTO CREDITS

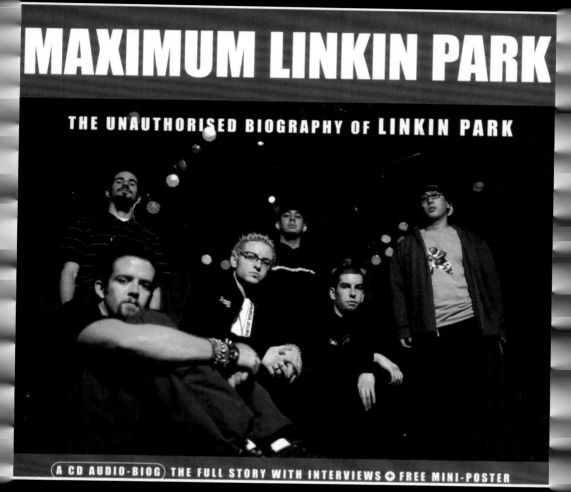